7 CONFESSIONS
for Supernatural MOMS

Tiffany MoniQue

Copyright © 2024 by Tiffany MoniQue

ISBN: 978-1-77883-342-7 (Paperback)

All rights reserved. No part of this publication may be reproduced, distributed, or transmitted in any form or by any means, including photocopying, recording, or other electronic or mechanical methods, without the prior written permission of the publisher, except in the case brief quotations embodied in critical reviews and other noncommercial uses permitted by copyright law.

The views expressed in this book are solely those of the author and do not necessarily reflect the views of the publisher, and the publisher hereby disclaims any responsibility for them.

BookSide Press
877-741-8091
www.booksidepress.com
orders@booksidepress.com

7 Confessions for Supernatural MOMS

Gratitude

This book is dedicated to my heavenly Father. It is because of His love that I have been able to embrace my identity and the revelation of who He really is. My many encounters with Him in the secret place have set a strong foundation in my life that has allowed me to continue to blossom into the mom that he created me to be. His voice has allowed me to cancel the false voices that tried to hinder me from walking in my purpose and owning my power. I am able to own motherhood with a fierce grace that looks absolutely good on me.

Thank you Papa!

To the amazing humans that made me a mom. You have changed my life and I am forever grateful. I may get your names wrong on a daily basis but each of you mean the world to me in your own unique little ways. You have developed in me eternal transformation that is priceless. I learn from you and admire who God has created each of you to be. I am literally living a dream by being your mommie. Jada, Jay, Janiiya, Journii, Jenesis, Judah, Jerusalem, Judea, Jahzneyah, Jordyn and Jericho I am rich because of you.

Thank You Babies

Foreword

For decades the definition of a mother has been defined by a woman's ability to keep house, prepare meals, and manage her children. It was deemed as the "American Way"! In the religious sector, motherhood is attached to the Proverbs 31 woman. But even there, you must portray those attributes to hold the prestigious title of "mother." Still in today's world, women continue to be sized up by the forever changing norms of motherhood.

Through her ministry of motherhood, Tiffany has demonstrated the many facets of motherhood. Confirming that seasons will be different with each childbirth, that priorities will shift, change will happen, and sacrifice will be needed - but through it all, the Lord will be constant, a mainstay. Like the wind, the pressure of motherhood will be determined by the highs and lows of life.

Tiffany through her grounded faith has weathered the storms around her and has never allowed them to be within her, no matter how great the pressure. I have been blessed to walk with Tiffany through several of her children's births and witness the unconditional nurturing and love, patience, obedience, and faith that it takes to answer this call of ministry. Trusting God every step of the way, she never wavered nor questioned the Lord's intentions, even when life didn't align with His plan.

Tiffany made the bold decision to not succumb to the opinions of others who judged through social economic lenses. It was in those moments where the Lord would elevate her gifts and talents to give hope to others. I watched the evolution of motherhood through Tiff's organizational systems, gifted meal plans and catering skills, her homeschool education program-founded on Christian principles and worship, and her business sense to manage her home as her family grew. Every gift she carries has been transferred to every child, depositing the seeds of faith, and developing in them a Kingdom Mindset. Her children's names reflect their seasons and the ministry that was birthed through them. They are a reflection of God's infinite love for a woman and the ministry of motherhood that He has called us to!

Tiffany owns her heavenly birth rights and kingdom citizenship. Through her desire to please the Lord, she challenges women daily to seek the Lord's true plan for our lives, even when it doesn't align with the one we have written. Through her own walk of salvation and ministry of motherhood she shows us what it is like to truly walk in obedience with the Lord, embrace the assignment that confirms your family is your first ministry, and trust God when parenting brings the ultimate sacrifice of your own dreams.

As a mother of a smaller tribe, I have been challenged and encouraged by Tiffany's personal ministry of mothering. She has redefined motherhood and what it means to care for the precious gifts that the Lord has entrusted to you. She reminds us that we cannot just care for the basic human needs of our children, but to also nurture their spiritual beings. Putting in them the language of worship, the posture of obedience (first to the Lord), the love of Christ, and the walk of salvation. -Tynisha Garner

Foreword

My mom has been on a beautiful journey of growing her relationship with God and I am so grateful that I'm able to witness it. I have seen her trust in God and her love for his word grow into something that is absolutely extraordinary. Her desire to please God is evident in everything she does and the way she treats others. My mom has gone through so many rough seasons, but every time she has come out with a new revelation of God and His purpose for her life. She has become my biggest role model and my closest confidant.

The words that she has so diligently put into this book are not empty solutions that she just threw together without even thinking. They're her testimony of what God has brought her through and she is boldly sharing them to every woman who needs to hear them. My life has changed for the better because of the words my mother has spoken over me. She is teaching me what having a strong foundation in God looks like. She is showing me what a God fearing woman is supposed to live like. She is showing me what an unconditional, sacrificial love looks like.

      My mom is by far the craziest person I have ever met. She dances like nobody's watching, and she eats more cheese cake than anyone I've ever seen. But in all the craziness of our lives, her humility and her perfect imperfections have encouraged me and inspired me to rely on God in every area of my life. Not to mention the fact that she gave me her last name. What an honor!

With Honor, Your First Born
Jada MoniQue

Preface

I was 22 years old. Scared, disappointed and all alone. I sat in the office at a planned parenthood on 95th street in Chicago awaiting the results of a test that could possibly shift the trajectory of my entire life. Hoping and praying that the test returned negative, I had no idea that my life was about to change forever. I replayed over and over again why I could not possibly have a baby. According to my perspective and my distorted view of myself, if this test was positive it must surely be a punishment for my wild lifestyle and decision to walk away from the church. Clearly I was not aware of the passage Psalm 127:3-5.

The conception of my beautiful little girl was my saving grace. Before conceiving Jada I had lived a lifestyle of darkness for 9 years. I began to venture into darkness at a very early age. I was a freshman in highschool when I had my first full-fledged sexual encounter. From that moment forward I was completely dedicated and addicted to a lifestyle of sex. The more I ran from God the deeper I went into darkness and the more confused I became about my identity.

Thankfully I had come to know God at a very early age. My parents kept my sisters and I in church and although there are certain things about religion and tradition that hindered my walk with God, it is that foundation that I will forever be grateful for. After experiencing a decade worth of darkness out in these streets I realized that there was no way in the world that I was going to raise my daughter outside of the will of God.

I will never forget! I was about 3 months pregnant. I was struggling heavily with depression, shame and guilt. I was sitting in the pew all alone at my parents church one night. It just so happened to have been a bible study night where they held an altar call. I was a very tiny girl so my belly had already begun to pertrude. I hesitantly stood from my seat and made my way to the altar. That night I gave my life back to Christ making a vow to never walk away from the Lord again. From that moment everything in my life began to change. It has not been an easy journey of restoration. I am still on this beautiful journey but my 'YES" was the beginning of something amazing!

My distorted sexuality and perverted lifestyle was one of the root causes of years and years of guilt, shame and condemnation. Because of that guilt I believed with all of my heart at one point that I was cursed and would never be able to have children. I had been married to my first husband for 2 years and we were never able to conceive. Not to mention the countless number of sexual partners that I had before, during and after him. Don't you religious folks go judging me. This is my testimony.

At that point in my life I knew for sure that I was cursed. But I realized after giving my life back to Christ that that marriage and those relationships were never a part of my destiny. God had plans before the foundations of the world to restore that which once caused me shame and use it for His glory. Not knowing that 2 years after I would give my life back to Christ I would meet a man that God would give a vision to of having a large family and that God would allow me to be the source by which he would conceive those 10 amazing children. It still blows my mind!!!

People ask me this question almost every single day "how do you do it." My answer is and always will be the same. "It is by the amazing grace of God." Why He chose this spunky, fiesty, passionate yet broken girl to conceive 11 human beings, I will never fully comprehend. But one thing that I do know for sure is that if He chose me despite all of my mess and mistakes and He trusted me to be the mother of all of my children. He did not make a mistake when He chose you. You might be thinking "well girl I was not as messed up as you." Well the point still remains. God can use anyone.

I believe that we as mothers lack understanding and revelation of the power of motherhood and the authority that we carry as moms. Society has influenced us to value everything above our children and families and we have even begun to even devalue life itself. Deuteronomy chapter 6 not only commands parents to place a priority on our children and families but it also commands parents to make Christ the center of our homes. I believe that if mothers operated out of a kingdom mindset concerning their identity and the power of the family unit that we would see our families transformed.

Many moms are experiencing the opposite of what the Kingdom has to offer. Day after day operating under dark clouds of depression, oppression and stress. I can relate. Like I said before, it has been a long journey of healing, deliverance and breakthrough for me. It was not until I received the true revelation of God's grace and the revelation of the supernatural that my life began to shift. Once God began to take me on this journey with Him into greater dimensions of love, truth, power, freedom and joy I never looked back. I have been learning and growing ever since.

I would like to share with you some of the truths that brought transformation into my life in hopes that you would begin to believe these truths and allow the truth to set you free! That you would enter into a greater dimension of identity, power, and intimacy with God and that those encounters would not only liberate you but also your families. In many ways the liberation of moms will unlock the destiny of the family unit. So I declare that as you partake of these prophetic confessions you are entering into supernatural motherhood.

Table Of Contents

-A Pause For A Soul

Eternal Talk
{A Pause For a Soul}

John 3;16 For God so loved the world that he gave his only begotten son that whosoever believeth in him should not perish but have everlasting life.

It is my desire that this book reaches even the heart of a soul who has yet heard the good news of the gospel and of the amazing love of the Father. Or maybe even that soul that has strayed away from the arms of the Father but has yet to respond to the invitation to return. Truth is, God desires for you to benefit all of the blessings of being a part of the kingdom. Every single exciting promise that we will talk about is available to you once you have accepted Jesus Christ as your Lord and Saviour. Your soul is important to me and it is even more important to God. So is your eternity.

So let's talk about something very exciting. This bomb right here is going to blow your mind. You will never be the same after I share this good news with you. And that's my prayer. That after you read the heartfelt words in this book you are empowered to live the life that God has called you to live and become that amazing mother that God has created you to be. The transition all starts with this revelation. So please listen closely!!

There is a man that knows you intimately. He knows everything about you. He knows you even more than you know yourself. And y'all know some of us think we know ourselves so well. The depths of the love of God are incomparable. He views you and looks upon you with such love, pride and endearment.

You may be thinking to yourself "how could someone look at me in such a way?" That very question is from a place in you that has not yet accepted your imperfections and views love as a reward based on performance. But God's love is extended based on your position in the Kingdom. See, God does not see your sin, faults or mistakes when He sees you. When He looks at you He sees his son Jesus.

The things that have happened to you, the mistakes that you may have made, your flaws, weaknesses, insecurities, shame and fears are all invisible in the eyes of the Father. God already knew that you would need a saviour. He knew that you would be born into a world that is full of sin, that you would struggle and even fall into temptation. So He gave His son Jesus to die on the cross for you. Oh my gosh!!! Do you hear what I said?!

Jesus died on the cross. shed his blood. And resurrected again to redeem your life from the curse of sin and darkness. Listen, all of this good news is right in the bible. I encourage you to read it. Best book you will ever read! It also includes major promises and benefits for God's children. This book not only talks to you about your identity and what God has done to give you new life. The bible actually prepares you to live abundantly in every area of your life and prepares you for life in eternity!

John 3;16 For God so loved the world, that he gave his only begotten son, that whosoever believeth in him should not perish, but have everlasting life.

So I have a question for you today....."Will you believe?" Even if you do not understand it all. Even in the midst of your mistakes, brokenness, circumstances, and maybe even shame. Do you believe that there is a God waiting to love you? Wanting to heal? Forgive and renew you? Wanting to embrace you and walk with you on your journey of motherhood?

A love that you can now introduce into the heart of your own children. An eternal legacy that will outlast any earthly treasure that you may pass down. Are you ready to receive that love? Because he is waiting with open arms ready to usher you into the life that you were created to live. A life of purpose and significance.

This life may be a life that is formed by pressure and fire. But through it all has the hope of Jesus Christ to sustain you. A life where your position in the Kingdom is secured by the "Yes" that echoes from your heart and mouth today. And if you have strayed away from the Father, would you dare to believe again?

I was once lost, hurt, confused and ashamed. I knew only of this man through the lens of religion. Ignorant to the relationship that he desired to have with me that would allow me to receive his grace and mercy. I know how it feels to leave the fellowship of the Father in search of something that is not always able to be articulated or expressed at the moment. And I also know the amazing and satisfying feeling of safety, acceptance and blessings extended once returning home to his loving arms. Wherever you may fit in this eternal equation of your soul, will you choose to pray with me right now? Right here! This very moment all of heaven is standing still and is anxiously waiting for your "Yes."

This prayer will openly proclaim your position in the kingdom and will declare into the atmosphere your steps towards a new life in Christ that seals the destiny of your soul.

Dear Lord Jesus, I know that I have lived a life apart from you. I acknowledge my sins and my need for your forgiveness. I surrender my life to your plans. I repent of my sins. I turn from my old ways. And I embrace you as my Saviour. Thank You for your love. I establish a covenant with you today to walk with you all of my days. In Jesus Name, Amen!

Oh Snap Sis!! Do you understand the type of heavenly party that is being thrown for you at this very moment?! The bible says that the angels in heaven are rejoicing. It is truly a day to celebrate. And if I were you I would! Welcome to the family or welcome back home! Now we can talk about all the juicy and exciting plans that God has in store for your life and your assignment as a mother.

Luke 15:10 Just so, I tell you, there is rejoicing in the presence of the angels of God over one sinner who repents."

Jeremiah 29;11 "For I know the plans I have

for you," declares the Lord, "plans to prosper you and not to harm you, plans to give you hope and a future."

Confession #1

My Posture Of Praise Determines The Outcome Of My Day

~Proverbs 18;21 **Death** and **life** are in the **power of the tongue**, and those who **love it will eat its** fruit.~

~Psalms 113;3 From the rising of the sun to the place where it set's, the name of the **LORD** is to be praised.

CONVERSATION: As moms it is vital to the success of our day that we walk in our identity as a worshipper and lover of JESUS. That first LOVE is what will empower us to LOVE & enjoy our children. Let's face it! There are a million things that we experience on a day to day basis that causes us to question the validity of our hearts for our children. The moment we begin to abide in the secret place and allow our hearts to be arrested by our intimacy with the FATHER- is the moment we will be able to mother our children with a SOUND

HEART that remains full.

If we begin to enjoy daily communion & invite God into our daily tasks as a mom we will experience joy even in the mundane. Our emotions will be filtered from a place of JOY and our children can witness the sanity of a Mama who IS CRAZY ABOUT JESUS! Not just crazy...Lol!

Your ability to embrace the reality of who you are in Christ will posture you to receive the supernatural grace needed to be the mom that God has called you to be. Your intimacy with the one who created your children will cause all of heaven to back you up in your ministry to your children. The thought that you could ever be a mom without God is insanity. Motherhood is a ministry that is eternal. So it will take eternity Himself to have the victory.

Psalm 5:3 In the **MORNING** Lord, you hear my voice; in the morning I lay my requests before you and wait expectantly.

Psalm 113

1. *Praise the Lord, you his servants; praise the name of the Lord.*
2. *Let the name of the Lord be praised, both now and forevermore.*
3. *From the rising of the sun to the place where it sets, the name of the Lord is to be praised.*
4. *The Lord is exalted over all the nations, his glory above the heavens.*
5. *Who is like the Lord God, the one who sits enthroned on high,*
6. *Who stoops down to look on the heavens and the earth?*
7. *He raises the poor from the dust and lifts the needy from the ash heap;*
8. *He seats them with princes, with the princes of his people.*
9. *He settles the childless mother in her home as a happy mother of children.*

Praise The Lord.

Prophetic Poetry

I was drowning in the insanity of my routine.

Everyday seemed just as familiar as the day before.

*Unaware of what was within me
I seemed to be a monster to those closest to me.*

The screams and anger resonated from a time in the past.

A foundation that built something that would never last.

My fears screamed louder than my infant.

I lacked witness to the power that lies within me.

*Words that were spoken over me
Kept me in bondage to a reality that was*

never mine.

A fight fought before the foundation of time.

A victory defeating every enemy of weakness and grief.

My lack of identity kept me from being mommie to those who came from the innermost parts of my being.

I needed liberating!

I once sang a song.

It was a resounding sound of surrender.

My tears echoed to the courts of heaven as hell began to render.

The warmth of the Son erased the cold case of depression that haunted my inner peace.

The dark cloud that covered me disappeared into the serenity of His wings

I was free!

Everything that ever belonged to me unfolded in that moment- As I began to wrap my mind around this gift.

GRACE!!!

I opened up my hands and received that which was rightfully mine.

Time began to rewind.

With the light of life pumping in my veins my DNA was that of a queen.

I was redeemed!

That reality began to shift the world around me.

My ability to be the mother to my seed was a priority.

No longer defeated.

I embraced the grace to thrive and the world around me became witness to the God who created me.

So now, they confidently call me Mommie!!

Confession #2

GOD Is My Refuge And Constant Place Of Escape

Psalms 91;2 I will say of the Lord, "**He** is **my refuge** and **my fortress**, **my God**, in whom **I trust**."

CONVERSATION: A refuge & fortress are both places of protection, covering, hope and trust. As a mom I find it very REASSURING to know that, in my daily struggles I can always run to the arms of God for HOPE. In a world where moms are either committing suicide or harming their children as a result of their lack of revelation of the safety of the Heavenly Father- the message in this Psalms is much needed. The revelation and reception of this passage can save the lives of mommies and babies. Mama I encourage you TODAY to run to the FATHER during your TIMES OF NEED.

Take a moment, step away and express to him the concerns of your heart. He already knows, He is just waiting for you to invite him into your day. God is a gentleman. He will never force you into a relationship with Him. But He is also jealous for you.

Song Of Solomon says that He is our beloved and we are His beloved. That means everything that He is and everything that He has is yours. When you are in need of hope and a safe place allow GOD to be your REFUGE & FORTRESS! It's not what He does, it's who He is. Oftentimes we are tempted to carry the weight of motherhood on our own. We sacrifice our intimacy with God on the altar of busyness and we wonder why we are overwhelmed and exhausted.

I myself have made the mistake of putting my trust in my finances, my image and those things that I can see. I know you've never done that. I'm tellin on myself right now. For so many moms trusting God has become cliche and not actually a lifestyle.

Trusting God is vital to motherhood because God is the only person that we can build our lives upon. Life changes. People change. But God stays the same. If we are tossed to and fro along with everything else in this world we will never be able to model stability to our children.

If we are not able to introduce our children to God as our refuge and fortress they will lack true confidence when things around them shatter. When our children witness our decision to trust God in difficulty they will unconsciously develop a fervency that will carry them in life.

We must read our word in order to know who God is and why He is worthy of our praise and trust. Oftentimes the situations and circumstances that we despise are invitations from God for us to go deeper in our level of trust. He uses everything! Nothing in our life is wasted. And as painful as some circumstances may be, God desires for us to look to Him. To run to Him as our fortress and allow Him the opportunity to be our all sufficient one.

In the book of Psalm David cried out "what is man that you are mindful of him? God the creator of the universe. The master artist and great revealer of all beauty and truth is thinking about you. He delights in revealing Himself to you.

He finds joy in providing for you, protecting

you, healing you and loving you. If we continue to look to temporary things we will never know God in a way that is more eternal.

God is not interested in a one night stand. He wants a long term relationship with you that will allow you to tap into heavenly resources in every area of your life. Motherhood becomes supernatural when you have revelation of a God that is eternal.

Prophetic Poetry

I fainted.......
Every part of me was weak
The moment He held me
I knew I would never be the same

In His voice I supernaturally received
Everything that He ever had for me

His lips never moved
But He spoke to my soul
Something completely new

I felt every part of me
Being drawn into a reality that
Was on the inside of me

Every need suddenly became an attribute
As the beauty of my beloved
Covered my insanity

Ever so gently He wrapped me in Truth

The secret place of LOVE

Ministered to every broken part of my
youth

Immediately I knew
The Tabernacle
The Secret Place
Even The Shadow
As my refuge

I surrendered...

Failure melted off of my purpose
Like wax
As I watched the master
mold me like clay

My soul fell in love with my spirit
As the union of wholeness
Covered my life
Like a blanket

Confidence ransomed me
And I begin to stand boldly
BEAUTIFULLY

I was now becoming a heavenly
masterpiece

An epilogue of prosperity

When I arose to reality I was set free

Confession #3

Christ Is My Supernatural Voyage Of Peace

Philippians 4;7 And the **peace of God**, which passeth all understanding, shall **keep** your hearts and minds **through Christ Jesus.**

CONVERSATION: Peace was just a noun to me. It had not yet manifested into my reality. The lack of this heavenly attribute resulted in a level of depression that covered my life like a blanket. It touched everything. My marriage, my children, my identity, my finances, my relationships and even my posture of sonship with the Father.

I lacked the understanding of how to lean into this gift in the midst of all of the noise around me. The trauma that I was victim to from childhood had become a close rivalry with my peace and I found it easier to embrace the fear, the trauma, the depression and the chaos.

I know many moms who refer to temporary

fulfillment such as drugs, alcohol, and even over eating as their voyage of choice into desired peace. Never reaching a consistent state of rest rather returning day after day empty and thirsty for more peace. Striving in motherhood and other areas of life while God continues to welcome them on this beautiful voyage. A VOYAG OF ENJOYING the ETERNAL peace that only comes from God.

A voyage is not short. It is extensive and lengthy. Girl God has promised you a long life of peace in Him! God's peace doesn't wear off with sleep or other temporary pleasures such as alcohol or worldly escapes. We have a never ending supply of God's peace when we allow ourselves to be KEPT by God. As a mom YOU NEED PEACE! Trust me I know.

There will be days when fear, stress and anxiety will try to befriend you. The baby is crying, the bills are due and the house is a mess. I encourage you to allow your heart and mind to be kept by your revelation and intimacy with CHRIST JESUS. He is the cheapest and best therapist!

I am actually very familiar with the temptations of embracing something tangible to fulfill you. Our lack of faith in God's invible providence keeps us looking to what is tangible- what the eye can see and the hands can touch. God's word says that faith is the substance of things hoped for and the EVIDENCE of things that we CANNOT see. Sometimes blindness is beautiful!

This journey with God is like a boat on the sea embarking upon a long voyage. On this voyage the weather is very inconsistent and unpredictable. Some days you are met with clear skies and bright sunlight. However, other days you are faced with the seemingly debilitating stretch of dark clouds, rain and maybe even strong waves.

Ecclesiastes 11;4 says, whoever considers the wind will not plant; whoever looks at the clouds will not reap.

Sis! God wants you to keep your eyes on Him and not consider the storm around you. It is in intimacy with the Most High that He covers you and leads you into a place of supernatural peace. Jesus Christ has already paved the way for your freedom. It is through your knowledge and faith in what He has done for you that you may partake in God's beautiful gift of rest and peace. Do not make the mistake of prioritizing everyone and everything above God. It is by Him and through Him that you are empowered to THRIVE as a mom.

I Declare That God's Presence Is The New Peace!

Psalm 91; 1-16 NIV

1. Whoever dwells in the shelter of the Most High
Will rest in the shadow of the Almighty.
2. I will say of the Lord, He is my refuge and my fortress, my God, in Him who I trust."
3. Surely He will save you from the fowler's snare and from the deadly pestilence.
4. He will cover you with His feathers, and under His wings you will find refuge; his faithfulness will be your shield and rampart.
5. You will not fear the terror of night, nor the arrow that flies by day,
6. nor the pestilence that stalks in the darkness, nor the plague that destroys at midday
7. A thousand may fall at your side, ten thousand at your right hand, but it will not come near you.
8. You will only observe with your eyes and see the punishment of the wicked.
9. If you say, "The Lord is my refuge," and you make the Most High your dwelling.
10. No harm will overtake you, no disaster will come near your tent.
11. For He will command His angels concerning you to guard you in all your ways;
12. They will lift you up in their hands, so that you will not strike your foot against a stone.
13. You will tread on the lion and the cobra;

you will trample the great lion and serpent.

14. *"Because he loves me," says the Lord, "I will rescue him;*
I will protect him, for he acknowledges my name.

15. He will call on me, and I will answer him; I will be with him in trouble, I will deliver him and honor him.

16. With long life I will satisfy him and show him salvation."
AMEN!!!

Confession #4

Imprinted Into My Identity Is The Capacity To Be A Great Mom

Philippians 4;13 **I** can do all things **through Christ** Who strengthens **me.**

CONVERSATION: The moment that I found out that I was going to be a mom the enemy whispered into my soul a long list of inadequacies that I thought disqualified me from this beautiful calling. I felt that I wasn't smart enough because I carried whispers in my soul from my childhood that I was stupid. Those curses spoken over me haunted me even into motherhood.

I concluded that I was a failure and disappointment to my family and church community becasue I was having a baby out of wed-loc. And I certainly felt unloved because the father wanted nothing to do with me nor this new little life that was developing in my womb.

Fear had now become the foundation on which I built motherhood on and the enemy had a field day with that mindset.

I walked away from the church when I was 18 never desiring to return. I was raised in church but grew to hate christianity. I felt that if being a believer required me to be anything like the judgemental, angry, religious people that I encountered then christianity was not for me. Not everyone fit this description but it was enough for me to form a belief system that pushed me away.

Coming to know God as a child reaped major benefits in my life so I am forever grateful that my parents did the best that they could to teach me about God. However God was now going to reveal Himself to me in a new way. God says in His word "I will do a new thing" and the conception of my baby girl was the new beginning of a new relationship with God.

The bible also says that God uses the foolish things to confound the wise. That which I thought disqualified me and brought shame upon me God has used to rescue me from a life of darkness and usher me into my purpose.

Never despise your mistakes. Mistakes are the vehicle by which we grow and learn. The vehicle by which God can extend His grace and mercy to His children. Proverbs 24:16 says For a just man falleth seven times, and riseth up again. Falling and making mistakes is a part of growth as a mom. You will never tap into the greatness that is within you without making mistakes.

Every mistake is aligning your soul with your spirit. As you learn and begin to transform and mature in motherhood the more your life will supernaturally begin to flow from the realm

Of the spirit and not your flesh. In our flesh are all of the things that we believe disqualifies us from being the best mom ever.

However your spirit man is perfect. So as mothers it is vital that we learn how to intentionally die daily to our flesh and begin to live from the spirit

That is why the bible says that we must be transformed by the renewing of our minds. If you do not begin to think about yourself the way that God thinks about you, you will not become who God created you to be. As a man thinketh in his heart, so is he. You are literally becoming the person that your heart is telling you that you are.

Motherhood requires truth! The truth about who you are and how God sees you. That is the truth that will set you free and liberate you into a greater realm of motherhood. That truth is only found in God's word and in relationship with God. Who you are in CHRIST is vital to your reception of His unmerited and unearned- yet readily available and never ending GRACE. Grace is what empowers you to do with God what otherwise you cannot do on your own.

As a born again believer God has downloaded into your very DNA all that you need to do and be what He has called and created you to do and be.

The world tells you that you need that lastest baby or mom gadget. That you need to have a great education. That your finances need to be perfect and that the circumstances in your life need to look a certain way in order for you to be a great mom. Girl, I'm here to tell you that none of those things can determine or define the type of mom that you CHOOSE to be.

Look to God's word to define who you are as a mom and aim everyday to become that. Your very bosom was designed to be a place of safety for your child. Children are created and born with a heavenly intsinct to love you and desire your love. And you were desingned with a heavely instinct to provide that for them. Being that mom requires you to tap into who you are and to LOVE that YOU into becoming the best version of you.

Your KINGDOM IDENTITY is what will determine your Capacity! So look within, not without!

Confession #5

My Hands Are Anointed To Carry The Heart Of My Children

Proverbs 14;1 The **wisest** of women **builds her house**, but folly **with her own hands** tears it down.

CONVERSATION: She builds her home and children with GRACE and her words are seasoned with a tone of love. She guards her childs heart like a lion and is a place of safety for her child in times of need. This is a beautiful depiction of a mother whose heart is postured intentionally toward the heart of her children.

This world is becoming more dark and dreary with each day and the last thing our children need to experience is a parallell of the world in the eyes of their mom. They need to see a soft and kind yet tenacious and strong posture when in the presence of their mom. Your ability to steward your anointing as a mom will determine the stability and health of your childs heart.

As God's people we need to be sending children out into the world who are LOVED and who LOVE others! That"s when we will begin to witness a change in our world!

Far too often our children are subject to the emotional abuse of an angry and tired mom yelling at her child or cursing her child out as if they were an adult. Tearing that child down as every harsh word expressed out of her mouth becomes that mom's outlet and the childs worst nightmare. I am guilty of harsh words myself due to stress, overwhelm and a lack of Intimacy with God. And I declare that enough is enough! It is high time for the world to see Moms walking with an anointing to build up their childs identity as a result of her own confidence in the Mom who God has anointed her to be.

I don't think we talk enough about the power of our words. For years I have had to work hard to be delivered from some of the things that were spoken over me when I was a child. Word curses are like invisible prisons. No matter how far your child may try to go in life, if you have spoken negative things over that child those words have the legal right to hold that child captive and hinder them from excelling.

Unaware of the cause your child may find themself in cycles that they do not have knowledge, understanding or the spiritual wisdom or weapons to get out of.

Oftentimes as parents we make the mistake of parenting our children out of fear. Fear of our children becoming like us and making the same mistakes. Or we can make the mistake of parenting our children the way our parents raised us. All of us are influenced by our environment and those environments build strongholds in us and in our bloodline rather good or bad. I'm so glad that God loves us enough that He sent His son Jesus to set us free from those strongholds.

But there is also work that we as parents must do in order to fight for liberation in our relationship with our children. In order for us to experience freedom from those strongholds we must first become aware of them. We must acknowledge them and the cycles that they have caused in our bloodline and be willing to do the spiritual and even physical work to break them. Our children are worth the work of self-development and building ourselves up spiritually. Self-development as a mother should be never ending.

I am constantly growing in my grace as a mother by educating myself and building up my spiritman. The bible says that we perish for a lack of knowledge.

I did not have a very close relationship with my mother growing up. I am a highly sensitive person and my mother is not the most affectionate or emotional person. She did the best that she could with the knowledge that she had but she did not know how to speak my love language. So that lack of connection resulted in me growing up with a deficit of intimacy. So I looked for that connection in all the wrong places. If we as moms fail to tap into our ability to reach the heart of our children then the world most definitely will.

As a mom I have had to rebuild intimacy with my children from the ground up. I'm talking about pioneering new experiences, traditions and memories. This rebuilding has been very humbling as I have had to realize that there is a lot that I needed to be taught about motherhood. I realized that

I made and still make a lot of mistakes. But the beautiful part is that once God gently ushered me into a certain place of surrender and humility I was able to model a mother who is not perfect but serves a perfect God who Himself is in the perfecting business. That humility has reached a place in my childrens heart that my pride and desire to be perfect never ever would have reached.

I have had to unlearn a lot of things that were modeled to me and taught to me about parenting. This isn't a knock on my parents for the job that they did but we should always desire to be better than the generation before us and if we are afraid to address and discuss necessary changes then the cycles will continue. And the only thing that is really keeping us from these conversations is pride. For me and my house it's whatever it takes. My children will be better than me!

The word of God has a lot to say about our children. If we really search the scripture and the full counsel of God's word we will witness the affections and promises of God for them. God cares about our children and has always had them in His heart. Jesus said "Let the little children come to me, and do not hinder them, for the Kingdom of heaven belongs to such as these." If Jesus knew how to prioritize children in a culture that was contrary to His affections how much more should we be doing to place value on them. If God's word is full of promises for our children, how much more should we be declaring over them?

We as moms can no longer equate tangible and monetary gifts with time and intimacy. We must no longer prioritize everything else in our lives above our children. We must heal and mature into moms with healthy hearts who are confident in our ability to connect with the heart of our children. We must surrender to the hard work of building culture and legacy in our homes of value and self-worth. Change requires humility and grace is extended to the heart that is postured hubly before God.

So mom, if your heart needs to be healed I completely understand. I have spent countless hours allowing God to restore and rebuild my life. It is my desire to see my children whole and to pioneer generational blessings that has allowed me to surrender to the process. How much do you value the heart of your children? How much more do you desire to build a new legacy of love in your family? How much more do you want to allow your children to see a parallel between God's heart and yours as that love overflows into the heart of your children? It is time for us to master motherhood.

Prophetic Poetry

Without a word
I witnessed a death
that my silence spoke into her soul.
Unaware of the commotion in my heart,
I struggled to conjure up the intimacy
to speak what I knew she needed.
Dying an emotional death
I began to project my neglect
upon my own seed.
I needed to be free!

It wasn't until
my heart was rescued,
that I received the key.
The key to release what
already held

HER HEART!

My seed was given to me
By the King who could see
beyond my being.

This King knew that my bondage

Would be the solution
to start a revolution
Of something brand new.

That the fight for my own
life would set a nation on fire.

This king's heart ransomed me
So that my heart could see.

I began to see the need
resounding loudly from
the soul of my seed
and as His love rescued me
my posture of humility
set my daughter free.

Talk about a heart to heart!

This right here
Is a masterpiece!
A beautiful melody!
Our testimony!

Confession #6

I Have Unlimited Access To Wisdom In Motherhood

James 1;5 If any of **you** lacks **wisdom**, you should **ask God**, who **gives generously to all** without finding fault, and it will be **given** to **you**.

Conversation: I will never forget my season of birthing boys back to back. God literally saw fit to give me Judah, Jerusalem and Judea all about a year apart. As if 4 girls and 1 boy weren't already enough. And then He did it back to back! I thought God had forgotten how hard I was working to finally become a sane mom. And now He wanted to add a bunch of boys in the picture. I had no clue what I was doing.

There are times in our lives as moms when we experience a situation that we cannot quite discern or comprehend. We desire clear understanding but we just don't know how to attain it. I have experienced this with raising my sons, raising a teen daughter, and even finding rest and balance as a mom.

I can remember the day that I spoke with their dad concerning my weaknesses and fear in raising boys. He told me that I had to understand them and treat them like boys and not treat them like their sisters. I began to apply that and instantly saw fruit. So I began to educate myself even more through books, blogs, conversations with other moms and the most important book of all. The manual to every area of life. The bible!

I have dedicated myself to personal development in order to raise these boys the way that God has desired me to. I didnt allow my fear and inadequacies to cripple me. I simply took it as an opportunity for more growth and knowledge. The moment that I began to SURRENDER to God these rough areas and ALLOW Him in, I began to experience such clarity that allowed me to witness SUCCESS in areas that I may have failed in had I not been willing to do the work. So I decided to keep seeking God's wisdom.

God PROMISES to give us wisdom

if we ask. And He said in His word that He will give it in abundance. As moms we can become too comfortable with inner dependency instead of becoming dependent on God. We will try our hardest to figure something out and look to every other avenue before we run to Jesus. Resulting in our insanity and continual struggle as moms. That's just crazy!

I know I have had enough. If you lack understanding just ask God. You may be a young mother. You may have not been taught how to be a mother. You may not know how to provide for yourself as a mother. You may not know how to parent boys or how to be intimate with your children. It may be a struggle for you to love your child. Or there may be a difficult decision that you need to make as a mom.

Whatever area of your life you lack wisdom or guidance in trust God and allow him to illuminate your path. Your dependence on God in a MOMENT will provide more wisdom and guidance than you can ever experience any other way. GOD'S wisdom is generous and never runs out! Oh yeah and it's free. Try it!

Confession #7

I Have Power To Take Dominion In My Home!

Genesis 1;26 And **God said**, Let us **make man** in **our image**, after **our likeness**: and **let them have dominion** over the fish of the sea, and over the fowl of the air, and over the cattle, and **over all the earth**, and over every creeping thing that creepeth upon the earth.

Genesis 1;28 And God **blessed them**, and God said unto them, Be fruitful, and multiply, and replenish the earth, and subdue it: and **have dominion** over the fish of the sea, and over the fowl of the air, and over every living thing that moveth upon the earth.

CONVERSATION: Okay Sis. I know what you're thinking! Girl I don't own any cattle and I don't even like fish..Lol! I get it! These scriptures may sound very outdated. But I'm telling you that this applies more to your life and echoes your identity as a woman and a mom more than you may ever fully comprehend.

First off- God is the same God yesterday, today and forever! So, the very same God that whispered those commands and promises into the identity and being of Adam and Eve is the very same God that crafted those very same instructions into your very being today. TAKE DOMINION!

I have a righteous indignation (that's a nice fancy spiritual word for angry) for the brokenness that we are witnessing in the family unit. Cycle after cycle we are left with the fragments of generational fatherlessness, poverty, divorce and even murder. Painting memories and beliefs into the mind of our children of dysfunction, chaos and disappointment. This is no judgement on anyone!

I myself am a victim of generational dysfunction and because of a lack of wisdom on how to take dominion over the spiritual warfare surrounding my life and family I began to establish those same cycles in my own home. There is a war for the family unit. Mothers are being attacked! Fathers are being attacked and our children are being attacked.

Satan is using the ignorance and weaknesses

of God's people against them while we continue to teach the same messages on salvation and sin. I'm not saying that the doctrines of salvation and sin are not important but I am saying that if we are going to ever see families being restored we must move beyond the milk of God's word and begin to feed God's people some good ole' meat!

Many people are not aware of exactly what level of power, authority and weight they should operate in in the spirit. The bible says in Ephesians 6;12 that we wrestle not against flesh and blood but against principalities. God is literally informing you that you are wasting your time fighting your husband, your mother-in-law, your child. Or whomever it is that you have found yourself in war with. What you are fighting is a battle in the spirit. Invisible forces of evil that try to distract you from their tactics and cause you to blame what you can see.

The bible also says that the weapons of our warfare are not carnal but are mighty through Christ Jesus for the pulling down of strongholds. Some of yall done threw pots and pans at your spouse and children thinking that you were going to get results that way. Again I'm not judging you I'm just judging your fruit. Trust me I have thrown a few pots and F-bombs in my crazy days. Don't you go judging me now!!! I've been delivered.

There are certain strongholds that are plaguing our families that God wants to reveal to us so that we may know how to pull them down in the spirit. This type of fighting brings eternal results for generations. How can you properly fight and defeat an enemy that you are not aware of? Winning the bible and taking dominion over what is rightfully yours require skill. It requires mastery. We need to become masters of defense and stop fighting against the enemy from a position of offense.

That type of war will require you to tap into that wisdom that we talked about. The bible is full of promises for you, your spouse, your children and your family. Promises and territory that God wants you to take dominion over. But you will never possess your promises or promiseland if you do not have revelation of who and what you are fighting against and what you are fighting for. If you do not embrace the powerful revelation that you are the seed of Abraham and that abundance belongs to you, then you will always settle for egypt. Egypt represents bondage. God wants us free. Our families belong in Goshen!

The bible says I have given you the power to trample on snakes and serpents. God is literally saying you keep praying to me about that crazy husband and those wayward children. Well I have equipped you with everything that you need to win the battle. Ephesians 1:3 says Bless the God and Father of our Lord Jesus Christ who have blessed us with every spiritual blessing in heavenly places in Christ. Every spiritual blessing refers to redemption, wholeness and every gift that believers receive by being united with Christ.

God's blessings on your life are a part of your identity in Christ. Blessings for the believer are not a need; they are an attribute. God created you to be blessed. You were made in the image of God. God is never in need. He has dominion over the skies and the ocean. The trees worship him in their movement and the birds sing of His praises. The bible says that the earth is His footstool.

Come on now girl! We were made in His

image so what does that say about us? Your family and children are a blessing and an addition to your life. Therefore you have what you need to care for and steward it with GRACE. Even as a single mother. Regardless of your circumstances that led to you being a single mother. Because God is YOUR father, his blessings will forever be upon your life. And he will empower you as a single mom.

The bible says in Psalm 68:19 that the Lord loads us with his benefits daily. So daily we have the responsibility as moms to go to our Father and receive everything that He has for us to succeed in that day. We literally have no excuse. We need only to have faith and obey.

God whispered into the existence of a woman the ability to look to the earth to provide everything that she needs as a woman and a mom. The earth is filled with unlimited resources for the success of your mind, body and soul. Which ultimately determines your success as a woman and a mom. We are without excuse! You may not have cattle in these modern times but you have a slew of kids. Or a spouse. And a home to tend to. There are things that God has entrusted into your hands that require your authority and dominion to be successful.

BE BOLD! Don't allow your home to settle in chaos. Call in your cattle if they are spiraling out of control. Set up your bait to reel in your little fish if they are in need of correction or guidnace. Love and affection. You have what you need to do it. It's a part of your identity and purpose. When darkness, grief, division, chaos, hurt, pain, bitterness, unforgiveness, betrayal, selfishness and any other spirits set themselves up in your home and in your life as a woman and a mom. Know that you have the authority to speak to that situation and command peace and clarity. To declare order and success. And you have the ability to seek wisdom and receive guidance. You have EVERYTHING that you need to Rock MOTHERHOOD with God's Grace!

Your realm of authority, peace, strength and even war is not mastered in the natural. No Sis, as a Daughetr of God your battles and blessings are won and received supoernaturally from the spiritual realm. It's time to ascend! That's a fancy word for go higher! If you are ready to thrive in motherhood, welcome Jesus into the journey.

Build a strong and firm foundation with Him and on Him and hold on to Him for dear life. Celebrate every single win, confess every fear, and reevaluate every loss and discover what you learned. Walk in humility. Never stop learning and growing. Posture yourself in transparency and giving so that others may gleam from your journey and watch your life begin to transform. Mothering in the supernatural will become a reality and your family and descendants will be eternally blessed. The seeds that you will sow into your family's life will be priceless! Motherhood will be a reward that will upgrade every area of your life.

Prophetic Word From The Lord
April 22, 2022 11;59pm

HOMES ARE BEING REBUILT

I am coming for my remnant
And I am starting in homes
In families
The family is the genesis
Of everything
I am calling the heart of
Mothers and fathers
Back to me
If I can reach the parents
I can reach the children
I am reestablishing
My altar
In homes again
In families again
In marriages again
In your children again
The pain that you are
Experiencing in your family
Is not to harm you
It is to purge you
To awaken you
To cause you to look to me
Yet again
I make all things
work for my good
Even those devastating

Circumstances in your life
My desire is to deliver you
From that which
Has kept you
And your family in bondage
And the keys
Are in my word
You can not do it
In your own strength
On your own
Your labor will be
In vain
My desire
Is for you to bare
Righteous fruit
Surrender to my work
And my plans
Unless I the Lord
Build the house
You labor in vain
My plans are to see
An entire bloodline free
My plans are bigger
Than what you can see
They have always been
About a people
A remnant
Allowing me to do
A new thing
In them and their families
Allow me to build

A new foundation
A foundation void of religion
And tradition
And the things
Of the past
A foundation built
On my covenant with you
And your covenant with me
And your revelation
Of OUR identity
I am doing a new thing
And I am starting
In you

Proverbs 31;10-31 Message Bible

A Good woman is hard to find, and worth far more than diamonds. Her husband trusts her without reserve, and never has reason to regret it. Never spiteful, she treats him generously all her long life. She shops around for the best yarns and cottons, and enjoys knitting and sewing. She's like a trading ship that sails to far away places and brings back exotic surprises. She's up before dawn, preparing breakfast for her family and organizing her day. She looks over a field and buys it, then with the money she's put aside, plants a garden. First thing in the morning, she dresses for work, rolls up her sleeves, eager to get started. She senses the worth of her work, is in no hurry to call it quit for the day. She's skilled in the crafts of home and hearth, diligent in homemaking.

She's quick to assist anyone in need, reaches out to help the poor. She doesn't worry about her family when it snows; their winter clothes are mended And ready to wear. She makes her own clothing, and dresses in colorful linens and skills. Her husband Is greatly respected when he deliberates with the city fathers.

She designs gowns and sells them, brings the sweaters she knits to the dress shops. Her clothes are well made and elegant, and she always faces tomorrow with a smile. When she speaks she has something worthwhile to say. And she always says it kindly. She keeps an eye on everyone in her household, and keeps them all busy and productive. Her children respect and bless her; her husband joins in with words of praise:

"Many women have done wonderful things, but you've outclassed them all!" Charm can mislead and beauty soon fades. The woman to be admired and praised is the woman who lives in the fear-of-God. Give her everything she deserves! Adorn her life with praises.

www.ingramcontent.com/pod-product-compliance
Lightning Source LLC
LaVergne TN
LVHW051226070526
838200LV00057B/4622